MW00983210

Proud to be Dutch

Netherlands culture, history, and heritage

Deborah van Meuren

Little Dutch Girl

WONDERNESS PRESS

Proud to be Dutch—Netherlands culture, history, ad heritage, Volume 1
ASIN 9798498664101
Canada
2nd Ed.
© 2021 Deborah van Meuren (Little Dutch Girl)

Published by: Deborah van Meuren (Little Dutch Girl)
Distributed by: Deboah van Meuren (Little Dutch Girl)
Canada

Image credits:

1. Rasbak-CCbySA3.0
https://creativecommons.org/licenses/by-sa/3.0/legalcode

Contents

PSST!

You know that scrapy, back of the throat "g" sound that Dutch has? You know, the one that sounds like a cat horking up a hairball?

Well, in this book, that sound is represented by an upside-down capital g like this: ⅁

The Dutch Invented Orange Carrots

Several hundred years ago, if you went to the market to buy a bunch of carrots, they would be one of two colors—yellow or purple. The typical orange carrots that we enjoy today were only developed in the 1500s, and we have the Dutch to thank for that.

Huh?

That's right, the Dutch invented orange carrots. Carrots were originally wild plants native to southwest Asia. The roots—the part we eat—naturally came in two color varieties: yellow or purple. The Asians domesticated the plant, probably about a thousand years ago, and from there it slowly spread westward into Europe.

In the early days of carrot domestication, the roots were long, thin, tough, and had multi-forked roots. And they were somewhat bitter. By the time they reached the Netherlands, in the 1500s, some red and orange varieties had emerged. Soon a few Dutch farmers in the town of Hoorn, about 20 miles north of Amsterdam, began growing and developing the orange type.

The farmers of Hoorn gradually bred a thicker, sweeter, crunchier, single-rooted carrot, whose popularity has grown so much that today it is the dominant type of carrot around the world.

Some theorize that the Dutch chose to develop the orange carrot because orange is the national color of the Netherlands. Maybe. However, it is more likely that the orange variety was already somewhat less bitter than the other colors, and thus was chosen as the base variety from which to develop a tastier carrot. Whatever the reason, the ever-inventive Dutch created something that can now be found in just about any kitchen.

So, what happened to the other carrot colors? They're still around! They are still used in various countries, most notably France. There, newly developed red, purple, and yellow carrots—called *carrots Nantaises*—are quite popular.

Did you know?

The Dutch word for carrot is wortel, pronounced [VORE-tull]. It literally means "root".

Carrots Nantaises

Written in the wind

When you think of the Netherlands, one of the first things that comes to mind is windmills. Proudly standing tall throughout the land, these bastions of the Dutch landscape have, for centuries, formed the backbone of the country. But did you know that the windmills have an ingenious secret?

The wicks

The four arms of the mill are called wicks. Each wick is made up of a latticework of wooden slats. In addition, each wick has a sail—a large piece of rectangular cloth that can cover the entire latticework, or be rolled up when the mill is not in use. It is the wicks that are the key to the windmills' secret.

When a mill is in operation, its wicks turn in the wind. To anyone looking at the mill, it is obvious that the mill is operating and therefore open for business. However, the magic comes when the wicks stop. They stop ("rest") for a number of reasons. Most commonly it's because the mill is closed. They can also stop because the mill is broken or because the miller is on lunch.

Strong winds are another reason for stopping the wicks—the miller stops them on purpose because the driving wind would turn them so strongly that the mill could be damaged. Regardless of the reason, a resting windmill always has its sails rolled away.

A windmill with its sails open

And here is where Dutch inventiveness comes in. In days of old, people looking at a mill could see if it was stopped but they couldn't tell the reason why. Was the mill broken, or was the miller just on break? Should farmers bother bringing their grain in to be ground, or should they wait until another day, when the mill might be working again?

So dutch ingenuity took over, and an efficient, simple, and clever communication system was developed—a system based on the position of the wicks. If a resting mill had its wicks positioned in the shape of a plus sign, with two of them pointing directly up and down, the other two straight left and right, the mill was just resting—only temporarily closed. However, if the wicks were tilted 45 degrees so that they created the shape of an X, the mill was broken and would not be open for an extended length of time.

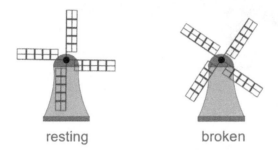

resting   broken

One of the beauties of this system was that since the dutch landscape is so flat, messages could be seen from several miles away. A farmer could tell immediately if there was any point in bringing his grain to the mill that day to be ground.

But the windmill's communication system wasn't just for business purposes. There are other messages it could send. If a happy event occurred, such as a birth or marriage, the mill announced it by positioning the top wick about 15 degrees right of straight up (at the one o'clock position). Similarly, sad events, such as a death, were signaled by tilting the top wick 15 degrees left of straight up (at the eleven o'clock position).

good news   bad news

Wicks in a bad news position, but with the sails open, signaled to everyone to come to the mill as quickly as possible. Flags on wicks in the "good news" position signified a celebration—perhaps the birth of a new prince, or a coronation.

Come quick!   Party!

Windmill Facts

- There are about 2,000 windmills in the Netherlands.
- Windmills always turn counterclockwise.
- Each windmill has a name.
- The oldest windmill in the Netherlands is the *Zeedam*, in the province of Groningen. It is over 500 years old.
- The tallest windmill in the Netherlands is *De Noord*, in the city of Schiedam. It is 108 feet high (33 meters).
- The Netherlands has a National Windmill Day, held every year in May.
- Windmills in cities are taller because their wicks needed to be higher than the rooftops in order to catch the wind.
- People have died by being hit by a moving wick.

The Water Wolf

The mother makes her way to the shed. Grabbing a shovel and pail, she calls to her young son, instructing him to follow her. The two climb through the fields and over the dike, making their way to the shore.

The tide is low. They walk out onto the exposed mudflats where the mother puts down the pail. She looks around, searching for air bubbles popping up through the wet sand, a sure sign that a clam lies below. Spying some bubbles, she begins to dig. She unearths the clam, then moves to the next likely spot. She continues along the beach, slowly filling her pail.

The boy busies himself on the mud. He stomps around in small puddles. He finds a large, orange-colored shell and puts it in his pocket. A flock of birds flies by, and he chases them, laughing as he goes.

The mother, tired from digging, straightens up and looks around. She sees the boy far out on the mudflats. She drops her shovel and runs towards him, calling.

"Come here!", she cries loudly. "Come here now!".

The boy stops and turns. He hears the mother and sees her arms beckoning him back.

"Hello mama!", he calls. "I am coming!".

He begins to run back towards her. When he arrives by her side, she grabs his shoulders and bends forward. "You cannot play out so far!", she scolds.

The boy looks up at her, bewildered. "Why mama?".

The mother shakes her finger at the boy and snaps, "If you play out on the mudflats the Water Wolf will get you!".

She grabs his hand firmly and walks back towards the pail and shovel. The boy hesitantly follows along.

After a few moments, he asks his mother, "Mama, what is the Water Wolf?".

The mother stops bends down, and looks the boy in the eyes.

Her voice low, she explains, "He is a dark, giant wolf who lives in the sea. Sometimes, when he is hungry, he comes near to the land and eats up children that have wandered out onto the mud."

The boy's eyes widen. A wolf in the sea! A giant wolf! He thinks for a moment, then an idea comes to him.

"Mama, if I see the wolf, I will run away, fast as the wind!".

The mother raises her voice.

"Listen to me! You cannot escape! He is quicker than the wind. No matter how fast you are, he will catch you!".

The boy falls silent. They arrive back where the mother left the shovel and her pail of clams. She collects them, and walks back toward the shore, the boy following her. They begin to climb back up the dike. When they reach the top, the mother pauses to rest.

While she catches her breath, the boy looks cautiously over his shoulder, back toward the sea. The water suddenly seems dark and uncertain to him. The clouds are moving quickly and the waves are growing larger. And there, far on the horizon, he thinks he can just make out a dark, moving shadow...

And in this way, in times of old, many mothers taught their children a healthy fear of the sea in order to keep them safe from the long, hungry fingers of the unpredictable water.

But the mother knows the Water Wolf is real. When the winter tides are high, and the cold storms blow in from the north, he awakens from his slumber. With ears low, and lips curled, he leaps over the land in great bounds, devouring everything in his path.

How to be a Frisian

Like any other country, the Netherlands has its share of stereotypes. For one thing, the Dutch have notions about what constitutes a "typical type" from each of the country's provinces. Let's take a look at some of those stereotypes by examining what the Dutch think a typical person from Friesland is like. Here is our guide on how to be a Frisian.

1. You must be tall

The people of Friesland are the tallest in the world. Adult males average over six feet, with many measuring even more. For comparison, the average for North American males is only 5 feet 9. While it might seem great to be tall, there is a downside. Frisians are constantly hitting their heads as they try to duck through doorways, their shirt cuffs only come to their elbows, and their legs stick out over the end of their beds so far that they can bend their knees and rest their feet on the floor.

2. You must know how to skate

And not just any skating will do—you gotta go fast! Frisians are among the fastest speed skaters in the world. Just look at the following Olympic Games results.

Total number of Olympic speed skating medals won for all modern winter Olympic Games (all years combined)

Rank	Country	# of medals
1	Netherlands	121
2	Norway	84
3	United States	68
4	Soviet Union	60
5	Germany	38

You can see that the Dutch are waaaaaay ahead. Okay, maybe not all of the Dutch medal winners were Frisian, but they probably picked up some of the Frisian greatness through osmosis...or something.

The Frisians love speed skating so much that every winter, if the weather is right (the canals don't always freeze enough) the province holds the Elfstedentocht—the Eleven Cities Tour [EL-uff-STAY-dun-tuɔt]. It is a skating race that meanders across the province and through its eleven main cities via the hundreds of miles of frozen canals.

The race itself covers 125 miles, and first place is typically achieved with times of about 6 hours, not counting the time spent at check-in points. Unfortunately, the last time the weather was cold enough to properly freeze the canals was in 1997. So now the province holds an eleven cities swimming race in the summer. No kidding.

3. You must be a farmer

Well, at least that's what other Dutch people seem to think. Now, there is some basis for this assumption. Friesland is, after all, a largely agricultural province, and an awful lot of Frisians have the surname *Boer* (farmer). And if their last name isn't Boer, it's some name that refers to the countryside or farming, like *Dijkstra* (from the dike), *Veenstra* (from the peatland), or *Akkerman* (field man). There are animal surnames like *de Haan* (the Rooster), and *Schaap* (sheep) and even food and plant names such as *Boon* (bean) and *Klaver* (clover).

4. You must love sheep

You really have no choice, because they are everywhere—in the fields, on the dikes, on the roads, in the living room...well maybe only on Sundays.

There are over a quarter of a million sheep in Friesland, more than in any other Dutch province. That's 200 per square mile. In a way, that makes sense, because Friesland also has more grassland than any other province. Power mowing all that grass would just be, like, really expensive.

5. You must speak Frisian

Tige moaie dei!   **Huh?**

And that's no easy feat. But, given that you obviously speak English if you are reading this book, you may have a head start, since English is the language most closely related to Frisian. Don't believe it? Here's proof.

English: That cow is eating white bread, butter and green cheese.

Frisian: Dut koe iets wyt brea, bûter en griene tjiis.

That'spronounced: Dut ko eets white bray-uh enn green-uh cheese.

Go back to Old English and the similarity is even greater. So, if you are ever in Friesland, try speaking a little Old English, and maybe some Frisian will understand you. Or they will think u r nuts and will run for the hills...which would take, like, a really, really long time (because the Netherlands is so flat...).

P.S. The cow said "Very nice day!"

The Dolmens of Drenthe

Tucked away on a sandy plateau in the eastern Netherlands lies the quiet province of Drenthe. A peaceful, largely agricultural province, it is home to large stands of natural forest and fields of purple heather. It is a favorite destination for Dutch citizens who want to "get away from it all". But they also come to see Drenthe's most famous attraction—the mysterious dolmens.

These rock structures, up to 20 meters in length, are scattered throughout the Drenthe countryside. They are the Netherlands' version of Stonehenge. The stones are huge—much too heavy for even a group of men to carry. They are placed in such a way as to create a long, narrow room. Two parallel rows of medium-sized boulders, half-buried in the ground, support much larger ones, which sit on top, forming a roof.

But who built these monuments? And why? Centuries ago, the locals developed their own answer to these questions.

> In ages long past, giants roamed these lands. They lifted these stones in place to create beds on which they could rest. Only such sturdy beds could support a giant, and only a giant could lift such stones.

True to the legend, the Dutch name for these structures is hunebedden [HOO-nuh-bed-un], which means "beds of giants".

13

But science tells us a different story. It has revealed that the dolmens were built by a people and culture now long forgotten. Archaeologists theorize that the structures, now often lying half buried in the ground and choked by trees and weeds, were originally built a few thousand years ago.

Unanswered Questions

Dolmens can be found in various countries around the world. In Europe, they are especially found in the North and in the British Isles, but they are particularly concentrated in Drenthe. Though of simple construction, the monuments would have required a fair bit of engineering to build: the largest stones weigh 20 tons each. How could an ancient people possibly have collected and lifted such stones? What was the purpose of the structures? And where did they get the stones from?

The last of these questions is the easiest to answer. During the last ice age, glaciers deposited large amounts of stone and rubble in the Drenthe area. Unlike most of the rest of the Netherlands, here you can find rocks!

But even though the rocks could be found locally, they still had to be moved to where the hunebedden were being erected—and the top stones had to be lifted in place. How a primitive people managed this is still unknown.

After the stones were in place, the gaps in between the walls were filled in with smaller stones, many of which have fallen away from the monuments over time. Once completed, the dolmen was used as a tomb. Inside, the remains of the deceased were safe from wild animals. The tomb also served as a lasting memorial, a way for those still living to honor their departed ancestors.

But not everyone agrees with this theory. They think the monuments were used for religious purposes, or as places to store food where it would be safe from wild animals. Many of the dolmens have not been excavated, so the archaeological evidence is sparse. Whatever their true purpose, they must have been extremely important to the culture that made them: no one would have gone to so much trouble to build them without a very good reason.

Today, the hunebedden are a source of pride for the people of Drenthe. An information center has been built in the town of Borger, next to the largest hunebed in the province. The Government has also renamed a major road in the province the *Hunebed Highway*.

A drawing from the 1600s, depicting giants building a dolmen

Dutch Santa lives in Spain

Say what?

That's right, no snowy, icy North Pole for every child's favorite man—dutch Santa spends most of the year in the sunny Mediterranean. So, what else is different about Christmas in the Netherlands? Well, just about everything.

The name

To start off with, the Dutch call the fat man with the toys Sinterklaas. Literally translated, it means *Saint Klaas* (which is where we get the name Santa Claus). The name Sinterklaas is a short form of Sint Nikolaas—Saint Nicholas. The original Saint Nicholas, who lived in Turkey in the 12th Century, was known to be especially kind to youngsters, and so has become the patron saint of children.

The arrival date

The excitement begins to build in early November, in anticipation of the day the great man will arrive—around Nov 15. That's right, in the Netherlands Santa arrives not on Dec. 25, but a whole 5 weeks earlier.

The helpers

Unlike North American Santa, who has gabillions of helper elves, Sinterklaas has only one assistant—Zwarte Piet (Black Peter). He is so named because his name is Peter, and he is, well, black. Tradition has it that the original Black Peter was an African orphan that Sinterklaas took in. Another tradition is that since Peter is the one who goes up and down the chimneys, his face is black from all the soot.

Although traditionally there was only one Zwarte Piet, nowadays, during the festive season, there are many. Dutch people (usually white) dress up in colourful costumes with ruffles at the neck and wrists, put on blackface, and follow Sinterklaas wherever he goes.

The vehicle

When the day arrives, families line up along the river front, hoping to be the first to see Santa's boat. Yes, boat. What else would you expect in the water-logged Netherlands? The boat slowly chugs into the harbor, with Sinterklaas standing near the front, and Zwarte Piets filling up the rest of the space. After the boat docks, Sinterklaas disembarks, mounts his white horse named Amerigo (yes, no reindeer) and rides around the town with his Zwarte Piets in tow, throwing candies to the excited children.

The outfit

Well, it's red and white, but that's where the similarity ends. Saint Nicholaas was a bishop, so he is outfitted with a bishop's gear—long red robe, mitre hat, and a long staff. He also wears a white lace apron. He does, however, sport a long white beard, like North American Santa.

Gift day

December 6 is St. Nicholas' Day. The night before, December 5, is known as pakjesavond (gift evening). Traditionally, Dec 5 was the day that Sinterklaas came to visit homes. Children waited excitedly for the moment he would come knocking on their door. Suddenly, there it was! Klop! Klop! They rushed to the door and flung it open. And there, in front of them, stood Sinterklaas and Zwarte Piet. If the children in the house had been good, the duo threw candies into the house, and the children scrambled to pick them up.

However, many children looked forward to the visit with mixed emotions. That's because of Zwarte Piet's large, empty sac. If Sinterklaas' list showed that a child had been naughty, legend had it that Piet would scoop him up, put him in his sack, and take him back to Spain.

But times have changed. Today, it is more common for children not to see Sinterklaas at all when he comes knocking. Instead, they just see the presents that he has left at their doorstep.

The stockings

But the fun isn't over yet! Sinterklass will visit a second time. Later the same night, Dutch children place one of their shoes (or a wooden shoe) beside the fireplace. Inside, they leave a carrot for Sinterklaas' horse and a card for the man himself. In the morning the children wake to find their shoes filled with candies.

The chimney

And how about the chimney? Well, Sinterklaas doesn't go down those—he gets his helper Zwarte Piet to do that. But he does travel from rooftop to rooftop via horse.

Santa's Home

On Dec 7, when all the hubbub is over, Sinterklaas goes back home. He returns back the same way he came, by boat, and spends the rest of the year in the warm climes of Spain. There he lives with his white horse, his black helper, no snow, and no wife (he is a saint, after all). But if you think the festivities are over, think again.

The Tree

Only after Sinterklaas has come and gone do the Dutch put up Christmas trees. A favourite decoration are wreath-shaped cookies. On January 6, all the decorations come down, and there are huge bonfires held at which all the trees are burned.

December 25

Traditionally, this was the day that religious Christmas occured. Families would go to church, spend some quiet time at home together, and eat a large meal. This day is called First Christmas Day. The following day, December 26, is called Second Christmas Day. On this day, many people take it easy, sleep in, relax, and have fun.

Santa's Third Visit

In these global times, the Netherland's has not escaped the influence of North American Christmas traditions. More and more families are embracing the practice of giving gifts on the 25th. This means that the kids get *three* days of presents: presents on December 5, shoes full of goodies on the 6th, and now more presents on the 25th. But it isn't Sinterklaas who brings gifts this time, it's the Kerstman (Christmas Man). This is basically the North American Santa. He's fat and jolly, sports a white beard, and delivers presents through the chimney. He doesn't live at the North Pole however, but in Finland.

The Wild Cattle of Flevoland

If you go walking in some of the Netherlands' national parks, you may be lucky enough to see some of the country's wild animals. Deer, foxes, wild boar, badgers and even lizards are not uncommon. But you could also come upon some creatures that are not quite what you might be expecting: wild cows.

Just to be clear, these are not black-and-white-spotted dairy cows that have escaped from some local farm and established a wild herd. They are honest-to-goodness, old-fashioned wild cattle.

In the mid 1900s, the Netherlands decided that it would be good for the environment to return some of the country's wild areas back to the way they had been hundreds of years before. The plan included re-introducing animals that had once been native to the areas, but which had long since disappeared. The idea behind the decision was that such animals played an important role in maintaining a healthy natural environment.

One such animal was the wild cow. Not seen in Europe for hundreds of years, the original wild cow—the ancestor of our modern domesticated varieties—was an animal called an aurochs. This is the cow of ancient cave paintings—a large, muscular animal with long, intimidating horns. Much larger than its modern-day descendants, a male aurochs weighed well over 1,500 pounds and stood five feet high at the shoulder. An impressive beast!

By reintroducing wild cattle to grassland areas of its parks, the Netherlands hoped that the balance of nature there would be maintained. It was expected that the cows' continual grazing and trampling of the ground would keep the grassy areas from becoming forest. In addition, their manure would be excellent fertilizer for the soil, which would, in turn, support lush plant growth. Insects, birds, mammals, plants—all stood to benefit from the cattle's presence.

However, there was a problem with their plan. The aurochs had become extinct in the 1600s. How then could the Netherlands possibly hope to re-introduce it?

As it turned out, the Dutch weren't the only ones interested in bringing back the aurochs. In 1930s Germany, two brothers named Heck had been breeding cattle with just such a goal in mind. By selectively mating cow breeds that had traits in common with their now extinct predecessor, the two men gradually developed a type of cattle that somewhat resembled an aurochs.

The new breed was called Heck cattle, after the brothers. Today, there is still some variation in the breed, with some looking much like modern day Spanish bullfighting cattle, others more like the Scottish Highlander breed. Whether the results of the breeding have produced an aurochs-like animal or not, this is the breed that was chosen by the Netherlands to repopulate its parks.

And so, in 1982, the Netherlands purchased its first herd of Heck cattle. The location chosen for release was a park called the Oostvaardersplassen [OAST-far-ders-PLUSS-un] (East Travelers' Wetlands). Located in the province of Flevoland, the area consisted largely of marshland and grassy fields. There were some wooded areas, but these were fenced off to keep the cattle in the grassland.

The cattle did well. Today there are hundreds in the park, and populations have also been established in other parts of the country. But the experiment has not been without controversy. The animals did so well that the park soon became overpopulated. The large numbers meant that there wasn't enough naturally occurring food to go around, especially in winter. Many of the cattle starved.

To help keep the population at a more reasonable number, the park began to cull the heard every winter, killing the weaker animals. Not surprisingly, protests sprang up. Some people felt that the park should feed the animals in winter, rather than let nature take its course. They also pressured the park to open up its wooded areas to the cattle in winter, so the animals could seek shelter among the trees.

The park did open up the woods, and they also built many small shelters throughout the park where the animals could get out of the rain and snow. But feeding the cattle was another question. The initial intent of the project was that the animals' numbers would be controlled by nature, not humans. However, in recent years, the park has been revisiting its policies and is now striving to find new ways to address the issues. In the meantime, the problem of overpopulation still exists.

What if you see wild cows in the Netherlands?

Keep a lot of distance between yourself and the cattle. They are not tame cows, but wild animals. They don't like people, are temperamental, and have big horns. They need space.

Heck cattle come in a variety of types. Some, like the one pictured here, look more like the Spanish bullfighting breed, which was one of the breeds used by the Heck brothers to develop their cattle.

Other Heck cattle, like the specimen above, look more like Scottish Highlanders, a long-haired breed from Scotland that was also used in creating the Heck breed.

The Netherlands: an Overview

The Netherlands lies along the north European coast, between Germany to the east and Belgium to the south. Originally, the word Netherlands referred to all the low-lying areas of northern Europe—the areas now known as the Netherlands, Belgium, and Luxembourg, as well as parts of western Germany.

In the center lies *Lake Ijssel*, called the IJsselmeer in Dutch [EYE-sull meer]. The lake used to be called the Zuider Zee [ZOW-dur ZAY] (South Sea). However, in the 1930s, after the mouth of the sea was completely closed off with a dike, the sea was renamed. It was named after the IJssel river, which flows into the lake.

Off the north coast of the country, in the North Sea, lies a chain of islands known as the Wadden IJlanden [WUD-un EYE-lund-en] (mudflat islands).

The provinces

Drenthe [DREN-tuh]
The name Drenthe comes from an older word, Trente, which meant three. The region originally consisted of three counties.

Flevoland [FLAY-vo-lunt]
This is the newest province. It was created by reclaiming land from the IJsselmeer. It is named for a body of water that used to exist in the location many hundreds of years ago, *Lake Flevo*. Back then, the area covered by what is now the IJsselmeer was mostly dry land. Lake Flevo was a wide part in a river which flowed to the North Sea. The word *flevo* is Latin for "flow".

Friesland [FREES-lunt]
The name of this province means "land of the Frisians". The Frisians were a large tribe of early peoples that used to live all along the northern coast of Europe, from Denmark to Belgium.

Gelderland [ꓷELL-dur-lunt]
This province is named after the city of Geldern which today lies in Germany. Several hundred years ago, before modern country borders were established, the entire region around the city was called Guelders. Much of this region lies in what later became the Netherlands. The modern city of Geldern, though in Germany, is very close to the Dutch border.

Groningen [ꓷROW-ning-un]
The province gets its name from its main city, also called Groningen. The exact origin of the name of the city is not known. However, hundreds of

years ago it was called Cruoninga and most probably was named after a local leader, whose name was likely Cruo, or Cruoning.

Limburg [LIM-ber-uhᵑ]
This province was named for a city of the same name. Formerly part of the Netherlands, the city, Limbourg, is now part of Belgium. The name of the city means "linden fort". A linden is a type of tree.

Noord Brabant [NORT BRA-bunt]
Brabant means "marshy land", or perhaps "newly broken land". Historically, it referred to a much larger area, part of which now lies in the province of Belgium. In fact, Belgium also has a province called Brabant, which is why the Dutch province is referred to as *North* Brabant.

Noord Holland and Zuid Holland [NORT HULL-unt] [ZOUT HULL-unt]
In the Netherlands, the word Holland refers only to the northwestern part of the country. Today, that area is split into two provinces—Noord Holland (North Holland) and Zuid Holland (South Holland).

OverIJssel [OWE-ver EYE-sull]
The name of this province means "across the IJssel". The IJssel is a river that forms part of the southern border of the province.

Utrecht [OO-treᵑt]
This province was named for its largest city, also named Utrecht. The name means "across the ford". A ford is a narrow part in a river that is a suitable place to cross. In olden times, the Rhine river narrowed here.

Zeeland [ZAY-lunt]
Several of the Netherlands' major rivers flow westward into this province, whose name means "sea land". Here, the rivers empty into a large delta area. The land in and around the delta consists mainly of islands and peninsulas surrounded by the sea, and these make up much of this province.

The first lapwing egg of the year

In much of North America, as the last grips of winter start to lose their hold, many of us eagerly await the return of the robin, a welcome sign that spring has truly arrived. In the Netherlands, especially in the northern provinces, it is a different bird that acts as the harbinger of spring—the lapwing. In country meadows you can hear its unmistakable call, *kee-veet! kee-veet!*, from which the bird gets its Dutch name, kievit.

But it is not the *return* of the lapwing that marks the beginning of spring. It is, instead, the discovery of the first lapwing egg of the year—we mean, the first egg in the whole country.

A hundred years ago, lapwing egg collecting was not just a quaint custom, it was a way to feed your family. Lapwing eggs were considered a delicacy, so much so that you could make a pretty penny selling them at the market. Each spring, in every northern city, town and village, thousands of lapwing eggs were sold, and for a hefty price.

This food was so popular that, in each town, the first person to find a lapwing egg in the spring received a prize. A special ceremony was held in which the finder would present the egg to the mayor. In return, the finder received a cash prize, and a certificate. The practice became so popular that, for a while, the first egg found in the entire country was given to the king/queen.

Then came the 1960s. Rising awareness of environmental issues and their impact on wildlife led people to question the effect that egg collecting was having on lapwing populations. As the decades passed, the tradition slowly declined in much of the country. However, in the northernmost provinces of Friesland and Groningen, still largely rural, the tradition hung on.

Between the years 1999 and 2013, the population of the lapwing dropped so dramatically (by 30%) that the government finally banned egg collecting throughout the country. Although the bird's population decline was largely attributed to loss of habitat and to farming practices such as early plowing of fields, the harvesting of eggs certainly didn't help.

However, the Frisians, determined to keep the tradition alive, found a way to continue the practice—but with a modern spin. Instead of collecting the first egg, they simply switched to finding and reporting it. In this way, the tradition remains, and so do the lapwing eggs. And the finder still gets a prize.

A northern lapwing nest. The eggs are almost 2 inches long and the mother always lays four of them. (*1)

August in times of old

Although the current word for the month of August in Dutch is *augustus*, in days of old the Dutch used the name oogstmaand—"harvest month". This was the month when the grains and vegetables in the fields were ready to be cut down/dug up and prepared for market or winter storage. It was a busy month but luckily often the driest of the year. This meant that farmers had many days that they could be out harvesting, making the most of the sunny weather.

Traditionally, the Dutch grew a variety of plants, but some of the more typical ones are listed below.

Grains

Much of the agricultural landscape was used to grow grains such as wheat and barley. The wheat was taken to the mill to be ground into flour. Barley was largely sold to brewers who used it to make beer.

Tubers

Tubers (root vegetables) such as potatoes and carrots were desired foods because they kept well and therefore could be stored to last throughout the winter. Sugar beets were a popular crop but were not eaten—their juice was extracted to make beet sugar.

Vegetables

Vegetables such as cabbage, brussels sprouts, and cauliflower were also common but could not be stored for as long a period of time as tubers. Kale, another common vegetable, would spoil fairly quickly, so its leaves were dried, and in that form it could last for many months.

Dutch witch trials

In North America, we grew up hearing tales about the Salem witch trials. But just where did the early settlers get the notion that witches must be burned? Turns out, they got those ideas from Europe.

The fear of witches goes back a long time. But, in 1400s Europe, that fear led to a whole new level of persecution. Equating witchcraft with devil worship, a campaign to root out witches began that lasted over 300 years.

One of the main driving forces was the Church and its enforcement arm, the Inquisition. In their fight against evil, they were particularly interested in rooting out witches. Anyone suspected of practicing witchcraft was tested and, if they failed, were swiftly brought to trial. Tens of thousands of "witches" lost their lives between 1450 and 1750.

There were even books written about how to recognize witches. The most famous was *The Witch's Hammer*, written in 1487 by a member of the Inquisition. The book outlined how witches could be identified and described practices the courts could use to prosecute and punish them. These practices included torture to elicit confessions, which, once given, condemned the person to a terrible death. Burning at the stake was a common method of ridding a community of witches, but not all accused died this way. Some were strangled, stoned, beheaded, or left to die in a dungeon. Some even died during torture.

Accused!

People were often denounced by their neighbors or acquaintances. Bad luck and timing were frequently the vehicles for arousing suspicion. A friendly pat on a dog's head could lead to accusations of witchcraft if, soon thereafter, the animal became ill. A person singing to themselves might, if seen from a distance, might be perceived as talking to themselves—or to invisible spirits. Sometimes, accusations were likely based on jealousy or spite, with the details made up. They could also be based on actual situations, with the details twisted. Not surprisingly, those with mental health issues were frequent victims. Outspoken women who "didn't know their place" were also targets. In some regions, there was a law that stated a dead tenant's belongings became the property of the landlord—a handy incentive for the landlord to accuse a tenant of witchcraft.

The Water Test

One of the most commonly practiced tests of witchdom was the water test. After the accused's arms and legs were tied, they were thrown into a lake, pond, stream or canal. If they sank, they were in luck—normal mortals were expected to sink. However, if they floated, it was a sure sign that they were a witch. This belief was based on the reasoning that witches must be lighter than regular people, since they needed to weigh less in order to be able to ride on brooms.

The Netherlands

The Netherlands did not escape the witch craze, although it was less severe there than in other areas of Europe. About 250 known cases have been documented, many occurring in the provinces of Gelderland and Limburg.

Perhaps one of the reasons that fewer people were executed as witches is the fairness and practicality that has long been characteristic of the Netherlands. For example, an accuser had to provide proof in court that the defendant was, in fact, a witch. Furthermore, the defendant could sue the accuser for defamation. If defendants could find several people who were witness to the defamation, and could get them to testify in court, they might very well be set free.

But perhaps the most unique way that Dutch people were able prove they were not witches was to make a trip to the town of Oudewater. There, in the justice hall, was a uniquely Dutch invention—the witch-weighing scale. People accused of witchcraft could have themselves officially weighed to determine if they were of normal weight, or if they were as light as a witch. If they passed the test, they were given an official document certifying that they had been officially weighed and that their weight was normal. They could then return to their hometowns, safe in the knowledge that, with those certificates, they had no fear of being tried as witches. People came from all over Europe to protect themselves by being weighed on the witch scale, which had been sanctioned by the Holy Roman Emperor, Charles V.

Towards the beginning of the 1600s, various provinces in the Netherlands began banning the water test. By the end of the century, a more enlightened, scientifically-focused Europe began to question the validity of witch hunts, and the practice gradually declined.

Witchy Facts

- The Dutch word for witch is heks.
- The last witch execution in the Netherlands took place about 1600
- The last witch execution in Europe took place in 1782.

The witch weighing scale in Oudewater.

Reclaiming land from the sea

Terpen

Much of the land in the Netherlands is at, or just below, sea level. Historically, this meant that the ocean waters regularly flowed over the land. With every ebb and flow of the tide, coastal land, and land along riverways, was slowly submerged, then exposed again, in a never-ending cycle. The Netherlands also receives a great amount of rain throughout the year, further adding to the amount of water on the land.

In order to survive in this environment, the Dutch had to develop various ways in which to manage the over-abundance of water. The earliest method used was the creation of large, flat-topped mounds of earth called terpen [TURP-un] (singular: terp). Houses, or even whole settlements, were built on top of such mounds.

During higher tides or storms, the inhabitants—and their livestock— were elevated enough to avoid being flooded.

The earliest terpen in the Netherlands were built about 2,000 years ago in the northern coastal provinces of Friesland and Groningen. The Dutch continued to build these mounds for about 1,000 years. Some survive to this day.

In this photo, the farm has been built on a terp. Although only slightly above sea level, a terp was high enough to keep the occupants safe from the sea in most weather. However, they were not high enough to provide protection from major floods. Today, flood threats are managed by dikes, not terpen.

Dikes

About the year 1000, sea levels rose permanently, and large areas of the Netherlands that had previously been above sea level were now submerged. The Dutch needed a new approach to combat the sea. It is in this period that dike building began.

The early dikes were no more than ridges of earth, and because of this, water and wind easily ate away at them. Over the centuries, building techniques improved. The edges of the dikes were strengthened by wedging posts deep into the ground all along the sides. The earth inside the dike was also interlaced with willow mats—bundles of willow twigs, tied together in a checkerboard pattern. These helped prevent the earth from washing away. Finally, grass was planted on top of the dike to further prevent erosion.

To ensure the ongoing maintenance of the dikes, each region elected a special committee, called a Water Board. It was the Board's job to monitor the condition of the dikes and to arrange for any repairs that were needed.

Dike building gradually overtook terp building and, after about the year 1200, became the dominant way for the Dutch to control the sea. Dikes were built along the coast, along riverways, and around cities and towns. A dike that formed a complete circle around a town or city was called a ring dike.

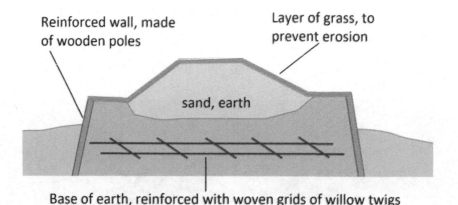

Reinforced wall, made of wooden poles

Layer of grass, to prevent erosion

sand, earth

Base of earth, reinforced with woven grids of willow twigs

Cross section of a traditional dike

Polders

The next advancement in the battle with the sea was the construction of polders—large sections of empty, soggy land, encircled by dikes.

Once diked in, the water that remained inside the polder, plus any new water that entered due to precipitation, had nowhere to go. In order to turn the polder into useable land, the water had to be drained out.

Draining was done by digging a series of drainage ditches inside the polder. These ditches travelled all the way to the dike, and right through it. During low tide, when the water outside the dike was lower than the water inside, these ditches were opened and gravity caused the water to drain out. In this way, bit by bit, the land inside the dikes dried out. Once dry enough, a process which might take several years, the land could be farmed or built upon.

Many polders, however, consisted of land that was below sea level. Because of this, the water level inside the polder was lower than that outside, even during low tide. In such cases, drainage ditches were of no use, as gravity would cause the water to flow *into* the polder, not out of it. To solve this problem, the Dutch began to use windmills to pump the water out. Mills built for this purpose, called polder mills, first appeared in the early 1400s.

By creating thousands of polders over hundreds of years, the Dutch reclaimed more and more land. Today, over 30% of the land in the Netherlands was created in this way.

Once one polder was created, new, neighboring land was also reclaimed. This was done not by building another circular dike, but by creating semicircular ones, which were attached to the side of ones that already existed.

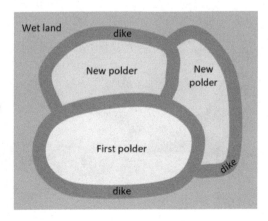

In this photo, the land to the right of the dike is polder land. The dike shown has a lane running along its top, a common feature. The lanes are meant for pedestrians and cyclists; motorized vehicles are not permitted.

Workers laying willow mats for the construction of a dike.

Sheep grazing along the top of a dike, a common sight in the rural Netherlands

In Other Words

Like English, Dutch has its share of sayings. Some are similar to ours, others are just, well, completely different. Here are a few to make you chuckle.

Van een kale kip kun je niet plukken
Literal translation:
You can't pluck feathers from a bald chicken
Actual meaning:
You can't get blood from a stone

Ik moet de aardapels afgieten
Literal translation:
I have to drain the potatoes
Actual meaning:
I have to pee (said by guys)

Appels met peren vergelijken
Literal translation:
To compare apples with pears
Actual meaning:
To compare apples and oranges

Hij heeft boter op het hoofd
Literal Translation:
He has butter on his head
Actual meaning:
He is being a hypocrite

Te veel hooi op je vork nemen
Literal translation:
To take too much hay on your pitchfork
Actual meaning:
To bite off more than you can chew

Ik ga horizontal
Literal translation:
I'm going horizontal
Actual meaning:
I'm going to sleep

Als de kalveren op het ijs dansen
Literal translation:
When calves dance on ice
Actual meaning:
When pigs fly

Van een mug een olifant maken
Literal translation:
Make an elephant out of a mosquito
Actual meaning:
Make a mountain out of a molehill

Geen twee kapiteins op één schip
Literal translation:
You can't have two captains on a ship
Actual meaning:
You can't have two cooks in the kitchen

When Napoleon ruled the Netherlands

In 1789, France broke out in revolution. Fed up with the oppression they experienced at the hands of the monarchs, they stormed the Bastille prison, freed the prisoners, many unjustly held, and proceeded to murder the nobility, including King Louis XVI, his wife, Marie Antoinette, and their 5-year-old son.

For the next 20 years, the country was in upheaval and at war with several countries including England, Austria, and Spain. In addition, France was trying to expand its borders, invading south into Spain, east into Italy and Germany, and northeast into Belgium and the Netherlands.

It was about this time that a young Italian was beginning his swift climb through the military ranks of the French army. Born *Napoleone di Buonaparte*, his father was a minor Italian aristocrat from Corsica, a large island 60 miles off the northwest coast of Italy. The island had been fought over for centuries, spending time under Italian and then French rule. For a time, it was also an independent state. The year Napoleon was born, it was taken over by the French.

When he was 10, Napoleon was sent away to a prestigious military prep school in France. At 15, he entered military college. At 16, he entered the French army. By the age of 24, he was a general. He was recognized as an excellent tactician and strategic fighter who won every battle he led.

So, when the new French Republic was threatened by royal supporters who wanted to put a King back on the throne, the politicians chose Napoleon to fight them off. The royalists were defeated, and Napoleon became famous—so famous that within a few years he became Emperor.

King Lodewijk I

A few years earlier, France had invaded and taken over the Netherlands. In 1806, recognizing that it was impossible to maintain control of all the lands under French rule without the help of those he trusted, Napoleon began placing his relatives in positions of power across the empire. He installed his brother Louis as "King of

Holland". Louis adopted the name of Lodewijk, the Dutch equivalent of Louis.

However, rather than simply keeping things under control, as Napoleon wished, Louis took it upon himself to expand his power and his independence from his brother. He wanted to live as a true king in his own right. He even turned the grandest building in Amsterdam—the city hall—into a palace for himself.

Louis was popular with the people and even tried to learn Dutch, although he was never very good at it. One story tells how he mispronounced "Ik ben Koning van Holland" (I am the King of Holland) as "Ik ben konijn van Holland" (I am the rabbit of Holland). The Dutch people joked about it for years afterwards.

Napoleon was not impressed with Louis' attempts at independence and in 1810, after several disagreements between the brothers, Napoleon forced his brother to abdicate. In his place he crowned Louis' six-year-old son as the new king. However, nine days later the Emperor changed his mind and dissolved the kingdom. The Netherlands once again became simply a part of France.

King Willem I.

In 1815, Napoleon lost the Battle of Waterloo and shortly thereafter he was forced to abdicate. The European powers, trying to redraw the borders and assign invaded land back to its perceived rightful owners, grouped Belgium, Luxembourg and The Netherlands together as one entity and granted it independence as The United Kingdom of the Netherlands. With this newfound freedom, the Netherlands eventually chose its own king: Willem I, who was a descendent of William of Orange. The new King's father had been the last Dutch governor prior to France taking over the Netherlands. Every monarch to rule the Netherlands since then has been directly descended from Willem I and is a member of the House of Orange.

Napoleon's Decree

In 1811, Napoleon enacted a law stating that:

- all people in the Netherlands must choose an official last name
- all future births, marriages, and deaths must be registered at the town hall

Up to this time, especially in non-noble families, Dutch people did not have surnames. Instead, they had what is known as a patronym—a second name that was the same as their father's first name. For example, if a man named Hendrik had a son named Jan, that son would be known as Jan Hendriks (essentially, "Jan, belonging to Hendrik"). Although this system helped somewhat in the identification of individuals, it caused much confusion, as many people in a region could have the same combination of first and second names. In addition, with each generation, a family had a new patronym.

Napoleon's decree stated that all men must choose a surname that would be the official surname of all his children and their descendants. If a father was deceased or otherwise not available, his father—the grandfather of the children—was to choose and register the surname.

A summary of the 1811 decree by Napoleon, making permanent surnames mandatory in the Netherlands, follows.

NAPOLEON I
By the Grace of God, and by the Constitution, Emperor of the French, King of Italy, Protector of the Rhine-Alliance, Negotiator of the Swiss Alliance.

18 August 1811—A Decree relating to those inhabitants of the provinces of Holland who, as of present, do not have a surname or fixed first name.

I - Those of our subjects of the provinces of Holland who, as of the present, do not have a permanent family or first name, are obliged to adopt such in the year of publication of this decree, and to declare these names before the city officials of the town in which they reside.

II - The names of cities may not be used as family names.

III - The officials are obliged to verify and swear to the authorities that each person's chosen family name fulfills the conditions outlined in these regulations.

IV - Excepted from the provisions of this decree are those inhabitants who already have well-known surnames, which they regularly use.

V - Those inhabitants who wish to conserve their family and surnames must, nevertheless, declare these names in front of the officials of the town in which they reside.

VI - The surname that the father, or the paternal grandfather should the father not be available, chooses, must be given to all children, who are obliged to use it in official documents.

VII - Those who have not completed the prescribed processes laid out in this decree, within the time allotted, and those who arbitrarily change their name in official or personal documents, will be punished according to applicable laws.

VIII - Our Supreme Judge, Minister of Justice and Minister of the Interior are charged with enforcing this decree.

Walking on the North Sea floor

Along the entire northern coast of the Netherlands, and eastward past
Germany all the way to Denmark, lies the Wadden Sea—the section of the
North Sea between the European mainland and the string of offshore
islands that lie just north of the Netherlands and Germany.

If you spend a few hours here, you will quickly understand why the name
wadden was chosen. The word means "mudflats" and at low tide that is
exactly what the sea becomes. Miles and miles of flats stretch out as far as
the eye can see. Ships can no longer sail the waters and must wait for high
tide. Even then, the sea is dangerous to navigate, as it is extremely
shallow.

At first glance, the exposed flats may appear to be made up of only mud,
but a closer look reveals their true richness. Everywhere are signs of small
marine animals, a necessary part of the chain of life. And the local wildlife
loves it. Birds flock to the flats to feed on the bounty that low tide offers. A
favorite meal consists of fat, juicy seaworms, which lie just under the
surface of the mud, ready to be dug up and swallowed.

The Wadden Sea is also home to countless seals, dolphins, fish, crabs, and other marine life, all of which rely on the sea for survival. So important is this area to wildlife, that it has become a UNESCO World Heritage Site.

Animals aren't the only ones that flock to the flats—people love them too. Intrigued by the wild, but temporarily "tamed" wildness of the sea, visitors come to experience the mudflats up close. They walk far out upon the exposed sea floor, marveling at nature and seeing what treasures they can find.

This activity is called wadlopen—mudflat walking—and a whole industry has sprung up around it. Guided tours—some walking, some by cart, buggy or horse—are commonplace. You can even walk from the mainland all the way to some of the offshore islands—a four-mile trek that takes four or five hours of slogging through thick mud and wading across various tidal channels.

Wadlopers—mudflat walkers—can only venture far out on the flats with the assistance of an experienced and licensed guide. There are two main reasons for this regulation: safety and environmental protection. The Dutch Government takes safety on the flats seriously. At low tide, the Wadden Sea is not simply one large mudflat. It is a complex network of mud, sandbars, and flowing channels of water. You must know exactly what you are doing and where you are going in order to avoid dangerous channels and to prevent yourself from becoming stranded. The Government is also serious about protecting the natural environment of the area. Much of the sea has been designated a nature reserve and people are not allowed to enter those areas.

An oystercatcher snapping up a sea worm

Deborah van Meuren

Taking an excursion with a professional tour company is a better, safer alternative. Led by an experienced and licensed guide, such trips will allow you to remain safe and to maximize your experience. The guide will also be able to point out and identify the various natural features and wildlife you may see.

These coiled strands are lugworm castings (basically sea worm poop). They indicate that a lugworm is just below the sand. At low tide, the mudflats are riddled with such castings and thousands of birds come to feast on the animals that made them.

A group of wadlopers

Dutch insights

Official Languages

The Netherlands has several official languages. Dutch is the official language throughout the country. However, in Friesland, Frisian is also an official language. In the Caribbean, there are 5 islands that belong to the Netherlands and, on one of them, there is an additional official language: Papiamento.

Size

The Netherlands covers about 16,000 square miles. Of that, 3,000 are actually water, so there are only 13,000 square miles of land. About 1,300 square miles (about 10% of the total land area) are still natural.

Population

About 17 million

Religion

No affiliation:	52%
Catholic:	23%
Protestant:	15%
Other:	10%

Deborah van Meuren

Miles of Road	About 86,000 (140,000 km)	
Miles of Dike	13,500 (22,000 km)	
Number of people killed in traffic accidents (2018)	People in cars: People on bikes:	233 228
Number of non-Dutch residents, by nationality (top 6)	Turkish: Moroccan German British Spanish Belgian	119,000 72,000 43,000 35,000 24,000 23,000

The Hoge Veluwe

Although much of the Netherlands is flat, there are some areas of slightly higher ground in the country. One such area is in the center of the country, in the province of Gelderland. Known as the Veluwe, this region consists of a series of raised sandy areas. The area around one of these raised areas has been made into The Netherlands' largest national park, the Hoge Veluwe [HOE-ɔuh FAIL-oo-uh] which means "high fallow land".

The park's history began in the early 1900s when the Kröller-Müller family bought up much of the land in the area to use as a hunting retreat. The entire property was fenced in and populated with large game such as deer and wild boar. They built a lodge to live in and a museum to house their art treasures.

In the 1930s, with the Depression in full swing, the family found they could no longer afford to maintain the property themselves. They donated much of their art and the museum to the government in exchange for a mortgage on the property, which they then turned into a charitable foundation.

One of the animals that park visitors most hope to see is a male red deer in full antlers

Moor is elevated land with moist soil rich in peat. Peat, the remains of rotted plants, is highly acidic and this, combined with excessive moisture, makes it difficult for trees to grow on moorland. However, low growing plants such as mosses and shrubs thrive. Heather, a pink/purple flowering shrub, is perhaps the most iconic moor plant. It is not one species but rather a family of plants. One member of this family, named Erica, is pictured here.

The antlers of the roe deer are small and straight, with only a few prongs. Measuring only two feet at the shoulder, this tiny deer prefers to spend its time in patches of heather where it can quickly hide should the need arise.

Wild boar are common in the park, and their numbers are increasing.

One of the game species the Kröller-Müller family brought into the park was the Mouflon, a type of wild sheep. This specimen is a fully mature male.

The park is one of the places in the Netherlands where wild cattle have been introduced. The animals can be temperamental and unpredictable and should not be approached.

In the sandy areas of the park, large sections of inland dunes occur.

The dunes are home to various creatures, including the sand lizard. Males are green, females brown.

Winter on the Veluwe means animals such as this red fox have to find ways to keep warm.

Much of the park is riddled with pathways. Exploring by bike is a popular activity, and numerous bicycles are available for rent at the park office.

To help keep plants from growing out of control, sheep are regularly grazed in the park.

The art museum is particularly renowned for its collection of paintings by Dutch painter Vincent Van Gogh, such as this one entitled "Wheat field with Cypresses".

Wild Boar on the loose

In 2015, there were about 5,000 wild boar in the Netherlands. By 2019, that number had doubled. While nature lovers are thrilled, others are not so happy.

Wild boar have always lived in the Netherlands. In fact, they are found throughout Europe. A favorite quarry for hunters, their meat has been common on European tables for thousands of years. But hunting has taken its toll on the animal's population. In the Netherlands, there were virtually none of the animals left by 1800.

But the boar was such a desired game animal that, in the early 1900s, Queen Wilhelmina's husband, Prince Hendrik, took it upon himself to reintroduce the animal to the Netherlands. He purchased several of the animals and released them on crown lands. The boar did well, and the population grew at a steady pace, spreading throughout the country. Since hunting was permitted, their numbers were kept to a manageable level.

However, everything changed about 20 years ago. Mounting pressure from citizens and nature organizations led to the enacting of a law prohibiting further hunting. Not surprisingly, wild boar numbers began to increase—and so did the complaints.

Boar eat a variety of foods. Plants include leaves, shoots, berries, seeds, nuts, fruit, and mushrooms. They also eat small animals such as rodents, frogs, lizards, or insects. Sometimes they will even eat larger animals, or their carcasses.

For most of the year, the boar live off the bounty of nature. Much of the food is simply there for the taking. However, when food above ground gets scarce, these animals begin rooting around under the ground for buried nuts and insects. With a massive head one third the length of their entire body, and powerful neck muscles, they can dig up frozen ground, break up old tree stumps, and even move large rocks.

In recent years, as their numbers have increased, so have their forays into human settlements. Feeding largely at night, they are especially attracted to garbage and gardens. Travelling in family groups of up to 20 animals, they can do a lot of damage in a very short time. Many a homeowner has woken up to find their garden in ruins, or the contents of their garbage bin strewn across their yard. Farmers' crops have also been damaged.

While dumped garbage or torn up flowerbeds are a nuisance, there are far more dangerous consequences of the boar's increase: traffic accidents involving the animals are on the rise. The sheer number of the animals means that the chances of one suddenly dashing across the road in front of a car have increased. With adults weighing between 200 and 300 pounds, hitting one can cause major damage to a vehicle and injuries to its passengers. Currently, there are hundreds of boar-related crashes in the Netherlands each year.

To manage the impact the animals are having on the country, the government has introduced a zero-tolerance policy for most of the country. That means that any wild boar are tracked down and killed. However, there are two areas that have been designated as safe havens for the animals—the Hoge Veluwe National Park, in the province of Gelderland, and the Meinweg National Park, in the province of Limburg.

In recent years, the numbers in these parks have been increasing rapidly. In 2015, the number of wild boar in the Hoge Veluwe National Park was estimated at 5,000. By 2019, it was 10,000.

So how does the Netherlands protect nature—the boar—and at the same time address the safety and nuisance concerns of its citizens? That's a question the Netherlands is currently struggling with. Various nature organizations are pushing for no shooting. They point out that the rooting around in soil that the animals do is a vital part of forest ecology, as it helps seeds germinate. But with burgeoning numbers, the negative impact of high boar populations, especially traffic accidents, is expected to grow.

The focus today is on trying to find natural ways to control the problem. In some places, fences have been put up to keep the animals out of certain areas. Some towns have erected fences around their perimeter and have found this helps. The government has also erected fences along some of the border between the Netherlands and Germany, to prevent even more boars from entering the country. The Hoge Veluwe National Park has large sections of fence along its borders, which helps keep the boar inside the park.

Boar bits

- Wild boar live to about 10 years of age.
- They have very poor eyesight but excellent hearing and sense of smell.
- Boar live in family groups consisting of females, this year's young, and last year's young.
- Mature males live alone and average about 3 ft high at the shoulder.
- Males grow four tusks at the end of their jaws, two on top, two on bottom. These are really just elongated teeth.
- During the mating season, males approach the family groups and fight for dominance and the right to mate with the females. They grow a thick layer of tissue under their skin to help protect them from tusk injuries during fighting.
- Wild boar meat appears on the menus of fine restaurants across Europe.

Boar piglets are born in March. For the first few months of their lives, they have stripes, which offer them camouflage. While they have these stripes, piglets are said to be "in pyjamas"

Deborah van Meuren

Amsterdam

Sometime before the year 1200 a small fishing settlement arose on the soggy banks of both sides of the Amstel River, near where it empties into the larger IJ River [EYE river]. Because the inhabitants had built a dam across the river, the village became known as "Amsteldam" or "Amstelerdam" (Dam on the Amstel).

The Amstel river was a key waterway for those to the south and west of the settlement, as it was the only way their boats could reach the IJ River, from which they could then sail to the North Sea, a rich fishing area. Because of its location along this route, Amsteldam soon established itself as a center of trade.

To help drain the settlement of water, canals, known as ring canals, were built around its edges. Their purpose was to have a body of water, outside of the city, into which excess water in the settlement could be pumped. The city was essentially a large island surrounded by a moat.

The ring canal system not only kept the city dry, but also produced new dry land within the city on which to build.

As the dry land inside the ring of canals was used up for new buildings, new ring canals were built further outside the town, allowing even more dry land to be developed.

Because much transportation was still by boat, even within the city, many additional, smaller canals were built to join each of the circular canals to each other at frequent intervals.

A 1600s drawing of Amsterdam, viewed from the Amstel River, south of the city. The city is surrounded by dikes, some of which have been reinforced with stone or brick. The river is very shallow, and smaller boats could be pushed along with the use of long poles.

AMSTERDAM.

Dam Square in Amsterdam. The square is located on the site of the original dam built across the Amstel, hence its name. The large building in the back is City Hall (later converted to a palace). The church in the back right is the Nieuwe Kerk (New Church). The dark grey building in the square, towards the right, is the old Weigh House, where merchants had their goods officially weighed. Once the City hall was converted to a palace, the weigh house was demolished because it obstructed the King's view from the new palace.

Many houses in Amsterdam are built right up against the water.

A 1500s map of Amsterdam by Cornelis Adriaenszoon. North is to the right. The large waterway running through the center of the city is the Amstel River, from which the city gets its name. Halfway up the Amstel you can see the dam spanning the river. The water along the bottom of the picture is the IJ river. The city is completely walled. Along the wall are numerous watchtowers and windmills, needed to continuously pump excess water out of the town. The many ships and boats, both inside and outside the city, attest to how busy a merchant town it already was at the time. The water along the bottom of the picture is the IJ River.

Originally, property taxes in Amsterdam were based on the width of the building. This is why there are so many narrow houses. But the lost space was made up for by building further back and higher up. The upper floors are accessed by means of steep stairs which make it extremely difficult to move furniture or goods into or out of the houses. To combat this problem, the houses were built with a special beam, located above the topmost floor, that extended a bit out into the street. The beam had a hook, from which a rope could be hung. The rope was used to haul items pulley-style into the house via windows. This system is still in use today. An additional architectural design feature was to build the houses on a slight forward tilt. This ensured that, when hauling goods up and down with ropes, the items hung freely, away from the building. This tilt can be seen in the picture above (building with open red shutters, and the building to the right of it).

To keep the water in the canals of Amsterdam from stagnating, a water movement system completely replaces all the water in all the canals with water from the sea a few times a week.

Built in the 1400s, De Waag ("The Weigh House") is one of Amsterdam's oldest buildings. It was originally one of the fortified gates that provided access to the walled city. As the city grew, its outer edges moved further and further away from the building. New walls were built along the new city perimeters, and therefore De Waag was no longer useful as a gate. At that point, the structure was turned into a weigh house, a place where bulk goods coming into and out of the city were weighed to determine their total taxes. Two hundred years later, it ceased being a weigh house and instead served a variety of other purposes including museum, archives, workshop, and fire station. Today it houses various organizations, including a restaurant on the main floor.

Bicycles are everywhere in Amsterdam, and throughout the Netherlands. The Dutch typically use cheap, second-hand bikes, as thefts are extremely common. Quality bikes are owned but are kept inside the house when not in use. They are not used for commuting and are never left unattended. They are used specifically for leisure bike rides or for athletic training.

Bicycle lanes can be found along just about every street in Amsterdam. The Netherlands is such a bicycle friendly country that bicycles often have the right of way over cars. At traffic lights, cars must wait several feet behind the white stop line, allowing space for cyclists to maneuver in front of them as they too wait—first in line—for the light to turn.

Amsterdam facts

- Because of its canals, the city has been nicknamed "The Venice of the North".
- The population is about 850,000.
- The average temperature is 63°F (14°C) in summer, 35°F (2°C) in winter.
- The city has over 50 miles of canals and over 1,000 bridges crossing them. Many of the bridges can be opened or raised to allow taller boats to pass.
- People often get rid of old or stolen bicycles by throwing them into the canals. Each year, the city removes over 10,000 such bikes from the waters.
- It is illegal to swim in the canals.
- It is illegal to urinate in the canals, unless you are pregnant.

The Lady of Stavoren

A long time ago, on the eastern shores of the Zuider Zee, a small seaport arose on the southwestern tip of Friesland, where a part of the land juts out into the water. It was a good location. With Amsterdam to the west, and German and Baltic Sea ports to the east, there were many merchant ships in nearby waters. Goods flowed into the town, and it became known as a good city in which to buy and sell merchandise. Many of the town's citizens became wealthy and, by the 1300s, the town was quite well known. It is here that we begin our story.

Once upon a time, in the rich sea port of Stavoren, there lived a greedy widow. She had so much money, she was not able to count it all. She had everything she could wish for: beautiful clothes spun from the finest cloth, sparkling jewels of every kind, and a palace decorated inside and out with gold and silver. She travelled in magnificent carriages led by the finest, fastest horses. She ate only delicacies and drank only the best wines.

But the widow lady of Stavoren was not satisfied. She wanted more. She thirsted for ever more exotic and unique riches that she could show off to the world. And so, one day, she decided she would send one of her ships to find a special treasure. She called for one of her sea captains and instructed him to sail the world in search of something remarkable.

"Bring me back the most precious thing in the world!" she ordered.

The captain bid his patron adieu and set off on his journey. For months he sailed the world, searching for just the right item. But, although he visited many ports, he could not find anything that the lady did not already have. He finally made his way to the Baltic Sea. There he met a man who seemed to have what he was searching for. It was golden, as precious as life, and something the Lady of Stavoren did not already have! Excited with his find, he returned home.

When he sailed into the Stavoren harbor, the Lady and all the townspeople rushed out to greet him. Word of the journey had spread, and they were all eager to see what treasure the captain had managed to find.

When he stepped on the pier, the Lady immediately barked at him, "Well? What did you bring me?".

"Oh, my Lady, I have brought you a most treasured thing!" he began.

"Well, what is it?" she demanded. "Quick! Quick! Tell me!".

The captain bowed and continued, "My Lady, I have brought you a whole shipload full of this precious item."

"Just show me what it is!", she snapped.

The captain slowly brought his fisted hand out of his pocket. He gently opened his fingers, as if he was afraid to break what he held.

When his hand was finally open, the Lady gasped in shock.

"Wheat? You bring me kernels of WHEAT?" she sputtered. "I demand to know the meaning of this!".

"My Lady", the captain explained, "it is the finest wheat in the world, brought from the fertile lands of the Baltic Sea. It makes the finest bread, which sustains our life.".

"Ridiculous!", the Lady snarled.

The captain continued, "My lady, we must have bread to survive, without it we cannot live".

By this time, the townspeople on the dock were laughing hysterically at the Lady and her captain. What fools they both were! The captain had hunted the world over and brought back only wheat! And the Lady, a snobbish, miserly woman, had been humiliated!

But the Lady was not finished. She turned to the captain and ordered him to sail out to the edge of the harbor and dump the entire shipload into the Zuider Zee.

The captain resisted. "My Lady", he explained, "it is not wise to waste such good grain. One day, if you are poor, you will wish you had such grain!".

"Me? Poor?", laughed the lady. "Bah!".

To make her point, she took off one of her rings. It was pure gold and set with large jewels. Yet, she tossed it into the sea.

"There", she said, triumphantly. "See that? There is as much chance of me becoming poor as there is of me ever getting that ring back!".

With that, she ordered the captain to dump the grain immediately. He saw that he had no choice and so ordered his crewmen to comply with the Lady's order. They sailed the ship out just past the harbor and dumped the grain.

A few days later, the Lady was sitting down for her evening meal. Before her was a plate of gold, on which lay a fine, freshly caught fish. It was beautifully prepared and smelled like heaven. She eagerly cut off a piece and popped it into her mouth.

"Ouch!", she cried, with her first chew.

There was something hard inside that piece of fish! She spat the food out onto her plate and gasped at what she saw. There, sparkling at her accusingly, was her ring.

You see, that fish had been in the harbor the day the Captain returned from his voyage. When the Lady threw her ring into the water, the fish had seen it and snapped it up. A few days later, that same fish had been caught by a fisherman, who sold it to the Lady's cook.

The day after the she bit into the fish, the Lady received news that one of her ships had been lost at sea. Then another, and another. Before long, she had lost her entire fleet, and her fortune with it. Poor and alone, she roamed the streets of Stavoren.

But the story does not end there. Shortly after regaining her ring, a curious thing happened. Out in the harbor, the grain that had been dumped began to sprout on the sea floor. It grew fast and tall, and its tips appeared above the water. The roots and stalks then began to trap silt brought by the sea currents. Before long, a large sandbar had developed. The sandbar was so large that it completely blocked access to the harbor. Ships could no longer reach the port. Many people of the town, formerly dependent on the trade the harbor brought, lost their livelihoods. So you see, it was not just the lady, but the entire town that suffered at the hands of her greed and contempt.

And that is how the once famous and wealthy city of Stavoren lost its prominence and became once more a small town.

This legend is based partially on fact. The city of Stavoren did indeed lose its trading status due to the development of a sandbar near the harbor. The locals called these sands the "Lady Sands". And further disaster lay ahead: In 1657, the entire town was swallowed up by the sea in a disastrous flood. The modern town of Stavoren is built on the new coastline that developed. The original town site is at the bottom of Lake Ijssel.

FREE!
More Dutch Tales

Want to learn even more about your Dutch Heritage?

I'm offering

More Dutch Tales

for free!

Just visit the link below to get 'em!

https://littledutchgirl.ca/more-dutch-tales/

Did you enjoy this book?

If so, would you please consider leaving a review on Amazon?

Even just a few words would help someone decide if this book is right for them.

And it'll help me bring you more books like this one!

Thank you!

More books.... →

Other books by Little Dutch Girl

Proud to be Dutch
Volume 2

**Dutch Legends
& Fairytales:**
Fun Folklore from
the Netherlands

Available on Amazon

Thanks for stopping by!

Made in the USA
Las Vegas, NV
16 December 2023

83000119R00046